Guess Who
Roars

Adivina quién
ruge

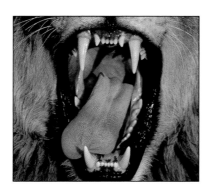

Sharon Gordon

Marshall Cavendish
Benchmark
New York

Can you see me in the tall grass?

---❖---

¿Puedes verme por entre la hierba alta?

I am a very large cat.

I weigh about 400 pounds.

❖

Soy un gato muy grande.

Peso como unas 400 libras.

I live in Africa.

My family is called
a *pride*.

❖

Vivo en África.

Junto con mi familia,
formamos una *manada*.

Our babies are called cubs.

They stay safe in our *den*.

Nuestros bebés se llaman cachorros.

Ellos están seguros en nuestra *guarida*.

I hunt at night.

I eat zebras and other animals.

❖

Me alimento de cebras y otros animales.

I can run fast.

I can move very quietly.

I can even climb a tree.

❖

Puedo correr muy rápido.

Puedo moverme muy silenciosamente.

Hasta puedo treparme a un árbol.

I see well with my eyes.

My hearing is even better.

Veo muy bien con mis ojos y mi oído es todavía mejor.

I am strong.

I have powerful paws.

I have sharp claws.

———————◆———————

Soy fuerte.

Tengo zarpas poderosas y garras afiladas.

Look at my long teeth.

They help me rip my food into pieces.

———◆———

Mira mis dientes largos y afilados.

Me ayudan a rasgar en pedazos mi comida.

18

I rest in the sunshine after eating.

I sleep up to 20 hours a day!

❖

Descanso al sol después de comer.

¡Duermo hasta 20 horas al día!

I have thick gold hair called a *mane*.

It is hard to see me in the dry grass.

---❖---

Mi pelo grueso y dorado se llama *melena*.

Es difícil que me vean entre la hierba seca.

But you can hear me!

My roar is like thunder.

Who am I?

¡Pero me puedes oír!

Mi rugido es como el trueno.

¿Quién soy?

I am a lion!

———————❖———————

¡Soy un león!

Who am I?

eye
ojo

¿Quién soy?

main
melena

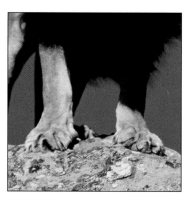

paws
zarpas

roar
rugido

teeth
dientes

Challenge Word

den A lion's home.
mane Thick hair that grows on a lion's head or neck.
pride A family of lions.

Palabra avanzada

guarida El hogar de un león.
manada Una familia de leones.
melena Pelo gueso que crece en la cabeza y el cuello de un león.

Index

Índice

About the Author
Datos biográficos de la autora

Sharon Gordon has written many books for young children. She has always worked as an editor. Sharon and her husband Bruce have three children, Douglas, Katie, and Laura, and one spoiled pooch, Samantha. They live in Midland Park, New Jersey.

Sharon Gordon ha escrito muchos libros para niños. Siempre ha trabajado como editora. Sharon y su esposo Bruce tienen tres niños, Douglas, Katie y Laura, y una perra consentida, Samantha. Viven en Midland Park, Nueva Jersey.

With thanks to Nanci Vargus, Ed.D. and
Beth Walker Gambro, reading consultants

Marshall Cavendish Benchmark
99 White Plains Road
Tarrytown, New York 10591-9001
www.marshallcavendish.us

Library of Congress Cataloging-in-Publication Data

Gordon, Sharon.
[Guess who roars. Spanish & English]
Guess who roars = Adivina quién ruge / Sharon Gordon. — Bilingual ed.
p. cm. — (Bookworms. Guess who? = Adivina quién)
Includes index.
ISBN-13: 978-0-7614-2466-6 (bilingual edition)
ISBN-10: 0-7614-2466-0 (bilingual edition)
ISBN-13: 978-0-7614-2386-7 (Spanish edition)
ISBN-10: 0-7614-1556-4 (English edition)
1. Lions—Juvenile literature. I. Title. II. Title: Adivina quién ruge. III. Series: Gordon, Sharon. Bookworms. Guess
who? (Spanish & English)

QL737.C23G6518 2006b
599.757—dc22
2006016816

Spanish Translation and Text Composition by Victory Productions, Inc.
www.victoryprd.com

Photo Research by Anne Burns Images
Cover photo by: *Animals, Animals*/Lewis S. Trusty
Cover Photo by: *Visuals Unlimited*/Barbara Gerlach

The photographs in this book are used with permission and through the courtesy of: *Animals Animals:*
pp. 1, 19, 29 (right) H. Pooley; p. 13 Animals Animals; p. 21 Len Rue; p. 23 Hamman/Heldring;
p. 27 Alfred B. Thomas. *Peter Arnold:* p. 3 BIOS (Seitre); p. 9 Gunter Ziesler; pp. 17, 28 (lower) Gerard Lacz;
pp. 25, 29 (left) BIOS (M & C Denis-Huot). *Visuals Unlimited:* pp. 5, 28 (top right) Barbara Gerlach;
p. 7 Will Trayer; p. 11 1992 G.L.E.; pp. 15, 28 (top left) Ksell B. Sandved.

Series design by Becky Terhune

Printed in Malaysia
1 3 5 6 4 2

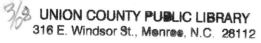